Mississippi

By Trudi Strain Trueit

Subject Consultant
Clay Williams
Director of Exhibits
Museum of Mississippi History
Jackson, Mississippi

Reading Consultant
Cecilia Minden-Cupp, PhD
Former Director of the Language and Literacy Program
Harvard Graduate School of Education
Cambridge, Massachusetts

Children's Press®
A Division of Scholastic Inc.
New York   Toronto   London   Auckland   Sydney
Mexico City   New Delhi   Hong Kong
Danbury, Connecticut

Designer: Herman Adler
Photo Researcher: Caroline Anderson
The photo on the cover shows a riverboat on the Mississippi River.

Library of Congress Cataloging-in-Publication Data

Trueit, Trudi Strain.
  Mississippi / Trudi Strain Trueit.
     p. cm. — (Rookie read-about geography)
  Includes index.
  ISBN-13: 978-0-531-12572-4 (lib. bdg.)   978-0-531-16813-4 (pbk.)
  ISBN-0: 0-531-12572-6 (lib. bdg.)   0-531-16813-1 (pbk.)
  1. Mississippi—Juvenile literature. 2. Mississippi—Geography—
Juvenile literature. I. Title. II. Series.
  F341.3.T78 2007
  976.2—dc22

                                       2006017608

CHILDREN'S PRESS, and ROOKIE READ-ABOUT®, and associated
logos are trademarks and/or registered trademarks of Scholastic Library
Publishing. SCHOLASTIC and associated logos are trademarks and/or
registered trademarks of Scholastic Inc.
1 2 3 4 5 6 7 8 9 10 R 16 15 14 13 12 11 10 09 08 07

You can smell the sweet
magnolia trees in Mississippi.

Magnolia blossom

The white magnolia is
Mississippi's state flower.
It is also the state tree.

Mississippi is in the
southern United States. It
is bordered by four states
and the Gulf of Mexico.

Can you find Mississippi
on the map?

CANADA

WASHINGTON

OREGON

IDAHO

MONTANA

NORTH DAKOTA

SOUTH DAKOTA

MINNESOTA

MICHIGAN

WISCONSIN

NEW HAMPSHIRE

VERMONT

MAINE

NEVADA

UTAH

WYOMING

NEBRASKA

IOWA

NEW YORK

MASSACHUSETTS

RHODE ISLAND

CONNECTICUT

NEW JERSEY

DELAWARE

MARYLAND

CALIFORNIA

COLORADO

KANSAS

MISSOURI

ILLINOIS

INDIANA

OHIO

PENNSYLVANIA

WEST VIRGINIA

VIRGINIA

Washington, D.C.

ARIZONA

NEW MEXICO

OKLAHOMA

ARKANSAS

KENTUCKY

TENNESSEE

NORTH CAROLINA

SOUTH CAROLINA

TEXAS

LOUISIANA

MISSISSIPPI

ALABAMA

GEORGIA

FLORIDA

ALASKA

CANADA

MEXICO

HAWAII

North

West   East

South

5

French explorers sailing down the Mississippi River with
their Native American guides

Native Americans were
the first people to live
in Mississippi.

European explorers arrived
in the 1500s and 1600s.
Soon, more people came
from Europe to settle and
farm the land.

Mississippi became a U.S.
state in 1817.

Mississippi is a Native American word that means "great river."

The Mississippi River is the largest river in North America. It flows through several states and forms the western border for the state of Mississippi.

The Mississippi River

Soil from the Mississippi Delta

The Mississippi River often floods. When this happens, the river dumps rich, dark soil into part of northwestern Mississippi.

This area is called the Mississippi Delta. The delta's soil is excellent for farming.

Much of western Mississippi is flat. It has swampy areas called bayous (BYE-ooz).

The bayous are filled with grasses, trees, and slow-moving streams. Alligators, catfish, frogs, snakes, and turtles live here.

An alligator in a Mississippi bayou

A Mississippi pine forest

Eastern Mississippi has low, rolling hills and pine forests.

Deer, foxes, rabbits, and squirrels make their homes here.

The Gulf of Mexico
borders part of southeastern
Mississippi. Crabs, flounder,
oysters, shrimp, and trout
live in the gulf.

Many people vacation
along the sandy beaches
in this area.

A shrimp

A highway destroyed by Hurricane Katrina

Mississippi's Gulf Coast is sometimes hit by strong ocean storms called hurricanes.

In 2005, Hurricane Katrina nearly destroyed Mississippi's Gulf Coast. People who live here are working together to rebuild their homes and businesses.

Jackson is the capital of
Mississippi. It is also the
largest city in the state.

Jackson was named after
Andrew Jackson, the
seventh U.S. president.

SCALE 1 inch = 50 miles

0   Miles   50

0   Kilometers   80

TENNESSEE

•Clarksdale

ARKANSAS

North
West ✦ East
South

Mississippi Delta

Mississippi River

MISSISSIPPI

✪ Jackson

ALABAMA

LOUISIANA

Gulf of Mexico

21

A Mississippi shipyard

Some Mississippi factories prepare meat and seafood.

Others factories make engines, farm tools, ships, and wood products.

Many Mississippi
farmers grow corn, rice,
and soybeans.

Cotton is also an
important crop.

A Mississippi cotton farmer

Exhibits at the Delta Blues Museum

A type of music called the blues got its start in Mississippi.

You can learn more about this music at the Delta Blues Museum in Clarksdale.

Maybe one day you'll
visit Mississippi.

What will you do first?
You can smell the
magnolia blossoms,
hear the blues, or simply
enjoy a sandy beach!

Visitors play in the sand on a Mississippi beach.

Words You Know

alligator

cotton

Gulf of Mexico

magnolia

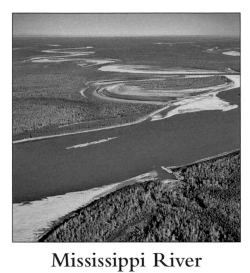

Mississippi River

ships

shrimp

soil

31

Index

About the Author

Trudi Strain Trueit is a former television news reporter and weather forecaster. She has written more than forty fiction and nonfiction books for children. Ms. Trueit lives near Seattle, Washington.

Photo Credits

Photographs © 2007: Airphoto-Jim Wark: 9, 31 top left; Alamy Images/D.E. "Mac" McGuffee: 3, 30 bottom right; AP/Wide World Photos/Rogelio Solis: 26; Corbis Images: 6 (Bettmann), cover (L. Clark), 18 (Warren Faidley), 29, 30 bottom left (Buddy Mays), 25, 30 top right (Owaki-Kulla), 17, 31 bottom left (Royalty-Free); Index Stock Imagery/Tom Carroll: 22, 31 top right; Minden Pictures/Konrad Wothe: 13, 30 top left; Visuals Unlimited: 10, 31 bottom right (Wally Eberhart), 14 (Glenn Oliver).

Maps by Bob Italiano